Conchas y Café Zine
Vol. VI, Issue 2

Cult of Personality

a DSTL arts publication

DSTL Arts presents

Cult of Personality

Conchas y Café Zine
Vol. VI, Issue 2

The work in this book was written by participants from DSTL Arts's Conchas y Café creative writing program, and first printed in February, 2021 by DSTL Arts publishing. All rights reserved. No part of this book may be reproduced in any form without written permission from the publisher.

Cover and Book Design: Luis Antonio Pichardo

ISBN: 978-1-946081-50-6

10 9 8 7 6 5 4 3 2 1

www.DSTLArts.org

Los Angeles, CA

Table of Contents

talky

Tina Fallon

Your community makes me laugh;

Zoey can make me cry in a Homeland.

I know some many useless things about you,

You don't even know.

There are so many times you have scared me

I can't sleep,

I toss and turn

With those images,

And yet,

I come back for more.

I tell my friends about what you shared,

To spread the word.

Some are thankful.

Some are… well,

They say they "just don't get it."

Sometimes you can get just too real.

Facts are hard to take.

I text my friends and they are all

Mr Robot.

The things you've showed me,

Real and scripted,

Consume me.

I like to share you with my loved ones,

But you are not more important than love.

You are just a diversion.

the electronic screen i love & hate

Karo Ska

the emails i check

compulsively while waiting

in line at the grocery

store, the text messages

i receive from friends asking

how i'm doing, the meditation app

i open every morning—the electronic

screen i love & hate, the tether

to a world outside

my four walls. access

to the electronic hive mind

curated by google

or facebook. a tracking device

for the fbi

where our location can be

triangulated at any time through

a ping to a cell

tower. attached to our hips,

next to our beds, within arm's

reach. dirtier than a public

bathroom, grease & germ

smeared—the electronic screen

we love & hate, the tether

to a world outside our four

walls. made from metals

mined from deep inside

the belly of the earth, constructed

in a sweatshop somewhere

in east asia where cancer

spreads how seeds scatter. everywhere

i go, i see people's heads

bowed low, eyes fixated

on lit-up pixels—playing

candy crush or tapping hearts

on a cousin's insta

post, scrolling through

a feed where they compare

themselves, wondering why

they haven't found

their perfect match or the money

for that perfect tropical

getaway, where they sip

mai tais or margaritas

on the beach—the electronic screen

they love & hate, the tether

to a world outside their four

walls. in the 22nd century,

where siri is now your only

companion, someone providing

virtual hugs as pulsations

through your body mimicking the human

touch—the electronic screen

you love & hate, the tether

to a world outside

that no longer exists.

Writer's Block Spins

Nery Martinez

My sad face reflects on my dark iPad screen,

As YouTube spins, spins, spins,

What have you done, what have you done, what have you done
    this day?

How much have you written,

how much have you written,

how much have you written,

To be one day closer of your daydream writer career, career, career

Why I Am Always Late To Class

Karyn Grasse

This piece was written from another lifetime, before the 'rona, back when we used to go places and do things. Remember that? It was nice to go places, and do things, but I had completely forgotten that it was also, at times, frustrating:

5:40

"Hey! I'm home!!! Oh, you're about to go to class, huh?"

"No. I mean, yeah. Yeah, I am. I just need to close my eyes for five minutes because I have a raging headache and I JUST took a Tylenol, and... I just need this headache to go away."

"Yeah, going to the chiropractor can release all those toxins into your blood. But... Anyhow... Baby woke up, do you want to see her before you go?"

"Oh. OH. oh... "

"Mmmmooooommmy... "

"Ok. Five minutes. Just five minutes to lie here and then I'll see baby and go."

5:52

"Hey, Baby!! Mommy's gonna go to class, OK? Give Mommy a kiss. Muah!! Love you Baby!!"

"I love you"

melt

5:55

"Hey, is it OK if I take Baby to KT Café?"

"Sure, sure, she can eat at KT. Do you need the eating stuff? Ok… eating stuff, eating stuff, where is the eating stuff? Here we go. Eating stuff AND diapering stuff—there! It's all on the counter."

5:59

"Oh crap! Water. Baby needs water. Where is the water bottle? Oh! Oh for the love of… ! This bib is FILTHY. Ok, another bib. Another bib… There! Oh, right… Shoes! Darn it, shoes. Hey, Daddy??? Remember her shoes!!!"

6:02

"Mmmmooooommmmy"

"Baby, mommy's busy."

"Mmmmmoommmmmy!"

"Baby, Daddy is RIGHT THERE NEXT TO YOU!!"

"Mmmoooooommmeeeee!!!"

"GET DADDY!!!"

"She got her foot stuck in the drawer, she got an owie."

"Oh Baby! Baby, Daddy will kiss it and make it better, OK???"

"Mmmmmommmmy?????"

"Ok, OK, OK!! I'll come up! I'm coming upstairs!!! Muah! There, Mommy kissed it and made it all better! All better, right??? Yes, all better!! Gotta go, Baby! Bye!"

"No!"

"Gotta go!"

"NO!!!"

"Muah! Love you, Baby! Hey… where's my phone?"

"You left it downstairs, by where you were napping."

"Oh! Thanks!"

-PING-

6:11

"I think your phone is in the office."

-PING-

"Behind the books."

-PING-

"FOUND IT!! Got it! I got it!! Okay, gotta go! Bye! Lock the door behind me, please? Back soon! Thank you!"

"Welcome."

6:17

-RING! RING! RING!-

"Hello?"

"You have the car seat in your car—"

"CRAP! Crap, you're right! I do!!"

"I'll come get it."

"No, I'm already turning around. I'm only a block away, be there in a sec."

"I'll come out."

"No, you'll leave Baby alone, I'll just drop it in front of the garage. I'm practically there. It will just take me a second."

"OK"

"OK"

"Bye."

"Ha! Bye! I think!!"

"Okay, okay, back on the road. We're back on the road! We are going! We are moving! Hallelujah!"

"CRAP!!! I forgot the cookies!! Ah!!!"

"Oh well… next time."

"Ugh!! WHY!! WHYYY is the stop light on Atlantic always SOOO SLOW????? Now I'm gonna be late!!!"

Song of Life

Lois Jackson King

True blue, just like an old shoe, sitting around just like you; don't
you have something else to do

Stand to your feet don't let the challenges of life and negative
thoughts bring to you defeat

Your life is not yet over; your cycle is not yet complete

Live life to the fullest; don't hesitate by waiting too late

Move forward in one way or another; choose your own lane, for
your future and for none other

Concentrate, on where you want to go; be your own best show

No need to wave banners, shouting with horns to blow

Satisfy yourself and be proud, time for you to make up your
own mind

And everything will be in its place; and all will be on time

Now all is bright and looking swell

And with God's help, you really can, do it very well

Inside a suitcase she packed
5 changes of cute and trendy outfits,
a honey yellow t-shirt with a pic
of a big Bee printed-on
and under it
the word Kind,
3 sets of shredded denim shorts,
a mint color dress
with a cute beaded bodice
she proudly wore that time
Mom and Dad
took her to ant Amber's wedding,
and a pair of black Jeans
with a Mickey Mouse t-shirt
Mom got her that time
they went to Disneyland
without Dad

Inside the suitcase she packed
a little bit-up
teddy bear she remembers
she has only
when she is scared

Inside the suitcase she packed
a blanket no longer her size
who cares when it helps
to muffle the sound
of late night fights

Inside the suitcase she packed
an old music box
with the song,
You Are My Sunshine,

a gift
  a gift Daddy gave her…

Title: Inside The Suitcase
By: Abraham Jaramillo

15

Object Control

Lois Jackson King

Mind is thinking and pushing, plowing, pounding away in my space

Meditating on positive things about what I would say

Deliberating which is correct, precise and presenting a negative

Object of past has taken residence in the now, and that's a fact

Reflections with restrictions is now the mode

Feelings of joy, happiness hindered, trying to unfold

The song, the song, oh the song, the object that brings a smile

My heart leaps and jumps as I recall Marvin Berry in 1954, maybe

too far back for some, and for others, it's been a while

"Earth Angel, Earth Angel, will you be mine; my darling dear, love
you all the time/ I'm just a fool, a fool in love with you"

Song full of hopes to be fulfilled, dreams to reach for and to gain

Song of future enjoyment with that special someone without shame

Song of encouragement, giving a sense of belonging, a great factor

Song with multiple worth and value to one's character

A song which regenerates my inner spirit and gives peace

A song which held true with a husband who is now deceased

JZ

Mauricio "Soul on Fire" Moreno

A pack of Marlboros

a day, the cheapest

whiskey a union man

could afford. A lesser man

would fall on his hands

and knees. A classic man,

die cast car models

adorning his studio

apartment. Gangster movie

posters and Braveheart mottos

plastered

onto asbestos

covered walls.

His steady hand

added coats of paint

to my mute wall,

nailed my
accomplishments,

hung my art to
his fridge, reminded me

of the wins I
drowned out for

my losses.
His steady hands

shaved my adolescence,
from my peach fuzz

to my mood swings, his stern
commands kept me

in line. i walked
in my stepfather's shoes

for 20 years, blackmailing him,
saving him, fighting with him,

18

helping him up 5 flights

of stairs, painting rich homes,

with him and still

i remember his pallid

smile, his rambunctious

stories, his unwavering love

of his family.

My Heartbeat

Felicia Taylor E.

A glimmer of hope appears through your presence

Majestic love, happiness

A flaunt of memory for the day, moment, time

I will not leave you

Your loss will not occur on my watch

Others may not see your life force, it's just a replication to them

Something to refer to as cute and adorable

You bring me more

My soul is rocked when I peer at you and step into your presence

I can not live without you

If fire consumes us, I will run to you

Hold you close and my shaky hands will come to your rescue

I'm puzzled when I enter spaces and importance's as significant
as you, are not dancing within it

How can you dismiss a lovely force

tickling and stroking memoirs of family and friend?

Allowing a new birth, a soul to be filled by you as they connect to your eyes and spirit

You are my heart beat

Ever present salvation and keeper of my dramatic and
homespun memories

My Sweet

Luz Donis

I chose you among so many,

having recognized you,

as soon as I walked through your door.

The warmth of your space,

like a familiar embrace.

Most of the family raved,

how perfect you were for me.

For a change I had no doubts.

Someone warned me, claiming you

would be high maintenance.

Another insisted you were too old.

Not believing any of it

I pledged myself to you,

then made an offer you could not refuse.

As it turns out you were raised

on a traditionally strong foundation.

Despite all the hardships, we have flourished.

The seeds I planted in your garden took root,

flowered and gave fruit.

Our laughter and music echo off the ceilings,

and footsteps off the floor.

Our Images and memories replay,

like from a projector on the walls.

Aromas of spices, oils and countless

guisados seep from the kitchen cabinets.

Finally, the scent of deep sleep,

dreams and tranquility flow from your rooms.

Mortar and brick do not mix with blood and bones.

I will pass on, my final good deed.

Grant your deed to those who carry on.

Latinx Gothic

Luz Donis

Poppy

David Fallon

Poppy's the name of the kid who lives next door to us. We call him Poppy because he laughs like the Pillsbury Doughboy whose name is Poppinfresh or Poppy for short. He's maybe about six or seven but acts like he's five. He lives right between my house and Mark Finster's house. Mark Finster is my best friend, and Poppy is definitely not. Poppy is the kid we make fun of and tease sometimes, but not all the time.

About a month ago was my eleventh birthday, and I got a brand new black and yellow Huffy BMX bike. The first time Poppy saw it, he spit right on it for no reason. I was mad for days and even hated him a while for that. But my mom says you can't hate people so I had to forgive Poppy. I'll never forget though.

Poppy has an older brother that everyone calls Dodge. I don't know why they call him that. Dodge is a teenager, which makes him very different from the rest of us. He really likes to pick on smaller kids. Once, he kicked my old bike so hard that the rim on the back tire bent. That's why I had to get the new bike. I never told my parents that he did it. I just told them that I crashed really bad. Mainly because Dodge said, "If you tell, then I'll have to rip your fingers off." And I really felt like he meant it.

Poppy sometimes tells me about the mean things that Dodge does. They have the only swimming pool on the block, so in the Summertime everyone comes over to go swimming. At least until Poppy's dad gets mad that we come over too much and yells at all of us to leave. Anyway, the pool always has a lot of little frogs floating in it every morning. Poppy says that Dodge gets the pool net every day and uses it like a catapult to throw the frogs against the back fence.

"They make a loud squish sound," Poppy laughs. Poppy sometimes goes to the fence to see if any of the frogs died from being thrown so hard. "But I never find none," he says sadly.

I can tell he doesn't like when his brother throws the frogs.

Dodge also does mean things to their calico cat, Snoopers. Snoopers is the nicest cat you met, to the point where he wouldn't even harm a mouse, but he's not good at getting away from Dodge. Dodge does what he calls "James Bond tests" on Snoopers. One of these tests was to tie plastic bags to Snoopers' feet.

"Snooper just laid down and did nothing," Poppy says wistfully.

Another test was to throw Snoopers in the deep end of the pool. Snoopers did something that time. He frantically paddled until he made it to the end so he could pull himself out and run under the house.

"He didn't come back for a hundred hours!" Poppy says in outrage. I'm pretty sure it wasn't exactly a hundred hours. But since Poppy is a littler kid, he tends to exaggerate things a lot.

The last James Bond test Poppy talks about sounds like it was mostly a goof. Dodge had a bundle of blankets that he said was Snoopers. He tossed it into the drier with a clunk and slammed the door. To Poppy's horror, Dodge switched the dryer on too high. Poppy ran screaming into the house for both, but both his mom and dad were at work.

"He said it was just shoes," Poppy halfway laughs, but you can tell he doesn't think it's funny.

Then Poppy tells me about the James Bond tests that Dodge does on him, like wrapping him in blankets and ropes and leaving him under the coffee table where he cannot move. When Poppy tries to yell for help, Dodge sticks a sock in his mouth. Only when Poppy is about to pass out from not being able to breath does Dodge finally set him free. One time he did this to Poppy, and Poppy thrashed around so hard he bangs his head on the edge of the coffee table. Poppy had to have five stitches on the back of his head.

Another test Dodge did on Poppy was to push him outside while he was still in his pajamas. He also threw out Poppy's blanket and stuffed animals. This was at the time when all the neighborhood kids were walking to school. Lots of kids saw Poppy standing in front of his house in his PJs. I missed it because I was still eating breakfast at the time. It was only after Poppy yelled so loud and banged on the door so hard that his mom finally opened the door.

About the worst thing Dodge ever did involved the frogs in the pool. Dodge had a habit of sitting on top of Poppy and tickling his chest and neck until Poppy laughed so hard he could barely breathe. One time Dodge took it a step farther and when Poppy opened his mouth to laugh, Dodge popped in one of the little frogs. Poppy nearly choked but was able to spit it out. That time Dodge got into really big trouble.

Mark Finster's dad has a super 8 camera that he sometimes lets us use. When we do get to use it, we make action films like "The Six Million Dollar Man," and my personal favorite, "Superman." I hold the camera while Mark stands there wearing a red towel for a cape with his hands on his hips. He looks out to the distance before running a few steps and jumping into the air. Then we cut to a scene of him flying, only it's not really him. It's my Luke Skywalker action figure with a piece of red fabric. We tie a string around him so that we can zip him around the yard with the camera rolling. It's pretty good special effects for a couple of eleven year olds.

I really like movies. My two all time favorites are "Star Wars," which I saw when I was seven, and "Emperor Strikes Back," which I saw when I was ten. The single worst moment was when Darth Vader said, "Luke, I am your father!" I think I almost had a heart attack, I was so surprised. And now we have to wait a few more years to see what happens next. I think waiting is one of the worst things for kids. We make Poppy do a lot of waiting when he wants to play with us, or wants to make movies with us.

"Later," we tell him. "We have big kid stuff to do." Saying that sometimes makes him cry.

The problem is, there are a lot of kids our age on the block but only one kid that's Poppy's age, and that's Poppy. He pretty much has nobody to be friends with.

Besides his age, the other reason we avoid playing with him is because his parents are super protective. Whenever they step out of the house, we know we are going to get in trouble. I guess I can't blame them too much. Sometimes we can do some pretty mean things to Poppy. Or at least things he doesn't like.

Whenever we play "G-Force," Poppy wants to be Jason who is the cool guy with the racing car, but we make him Keyop instead, who is the little guy who rides around in the bug car. We also made a pretend monster that we use to scare Poppy when we want him to go away. The Googla Monster is a green and purple goblin-like creature who lives at the school at the end of the block. All we have to do to get Poppy to run home is say something like, "I just saw the Googla Monster climbing those trees!" It pretty much works every time.

Mark Finster's dad is a really religious guy who tells us stories about the Rapture and how the end of the world is coming, and we will know when we are offered the mark of the beast and things like that. I always feel really uncomfortable when he tells these stories, like he is trying to scare me in the way that we scare Poppy with the Googla Monster. His dad also does strange things like eat peanut butter and pickle sandwiches, and makes his dog cry by yanking on its leash really hard. Sometimes I think he doesn't want me to be around Mark. A lot of times he tells me Mark is not home even though it's a Saturday, and where else would Mark be. When that happens, I get really lonely and even feel pretty sad. It makes me feel like no one likes me. When that happens, I sometimes go next door to play with Poppy and we even have some good times.

Poppy has a plastic train set that he loves to build on the garage floor. When I'm there, we use other toys to create large hills so we can turn it into a roller coaster. We look for all kinds of new obstacles and try to see just how high we can build it up. Poppy gets really excited when we let the train go, and he laughs hysterically when it inevitably flies off the track.

"Let's make it better, faster, more scarier!" he squeals in delight. And so we do. At times like this, I can't help but feel bad for Poppy. He's just a little kid who wants to have fun and laugh and play. So many people treat him badly, and sometimes I am one of them. But then Mark Finster will show up and I know I have to leave. It's just the way things have to be.

Soy Quien Soy. So.

Jessica V. Gonzalez

I am who I am

I am what you see

I is who I is

It's me?

I am who you want me to be

I am what you want to see

I am how you want to see me

I am who you allow me to be

I am them, when I am not a we

I am who I am

I am what I let you see

I is who I need to be

I am who I am

I can't help it, I am me

I was born this way

I am who I am

Who else can I be.

Mi Felicidad

Sanjui Martinez

Mi ventana a la vida,

mis discos de jazz y otros

para mi deleite ecléctico.

Mi taza favorita

inscrita con letras rosadas

con mi bebida alentadora.

La puesta del sol,

las olas del mar,

como llamando

   mi nombre,

juegan con la arena

y la traen a mis pies

mientras las alegres gaviotas

alimentan mi alma,

y en mi mano

tinta negra, azul, y roja,

o un simple lápiz

marcando en cuaderno

      de raya

los versos que me han de

inmortalizar.

Mi felicidad

Delectable Collectables

Michelle Smith

The Hands of Grandma

Lois Jackson King

The beautiful hands of grandma were strong and hard working

Grandma's hands didn't have to labor but her desire to mentor
to me the gift of pride

And her love she had was shown through the work of her hands,
she did not hide

Oh those hands, hands of grandma, are no longer here

But in many areas of my life, grandma's hands do appear

Grandma's hands took me to church; taught me just how to pray

She said to me, in God's word I must always stay

Grandma's hands cooked those good tasting meals

They were much better tasting than those meals on wheels

Grandma's hands made me say ouch when I had done
something wrong

Oh how I miss those hands that were worn and wrinkled and strong

Because of the washing of clothes and those pots and pans

Her hands could be warm and gentle and stern

The hands of grandma kept me from making many wrong turns

Oh bless the hands of grandmas everywhere

The hands of grandmas, who could show how much they
really cared

Hands may come and hands may go

The hands of my grandma gave to me a special glow

Silver Life

Felicia Taylor E.

Plain silver rimmed glasses on the bedside table, next to tissue
and nail clippers always near by

No reading material that will be read, except for the weekly
circular of the grocery stores

Particularly the $5 Vons Friday sale

An earplug in his ear to hear the sports stats of the Cowboys or
any sports info out there

Bare feet that hit upon a wooden floor, sometimes covered with
thick cotton socks

And a warm pair of comfy pants on that he's worn out

No color of shoes in particular, just those of comfort for the day
from heel to toe

A sneeze before bedtime and at night

Few cups of coffee to help him not doze

The only particulars required of this?

Creamed nicely, piping hot, with a

medium sugar amount

Work toil from morn till night

Sunday is church is a Family together break

Zones in on a few shows that are of note, and repeats his favorites
like Karate Kid

and the 5 Rocky shows

Eats a Ribeye steak, he says is "cooked perfectly by my wife,"
for his Birthday breakfast and sometimes Fathers Day

2 fried eggs done 'medium to hard' is his

desired taste

His time away from work is spent helping his son with school
and giving support to his wife

In rarity, his joy is a cold brew, specialty Hot wings and his
barbecueing of all meats in the house

Simplicity of life and joyful times,

with bills that are paid, is what matters most

With understanding that when this is all gone, that we move on
and that's life's way

Hello

Michelle Smith

KH

Mauricio "Soul on Fire" Moreno

In the morning, she washes her

hands. Reads aloud

her father's text to her current

lover. Makes breakfast

for one,

blasts OneRepublic,

'I Lived', lights a Newport

100, gets on

the 405, parks the car

rear-in, sprays the car

with Victoria's Secret

perfume, and heads

into work. At work,

she washes her

hands. Deletes her father's

text, asking to see him

today. Answers her e-mails,

signs them off

with her new title, chats

with her colleagues

about 'Scandal,' waits

until lunchtime to reply

to the angry e-mail

requesting a follow-up. At lunch,

she washes her

hands. Complains

about the angry e-mail

to a colleague, any colleague, asks

about their day, continues

complaining, checks her phone

for a text. After work,

she washes her

hands. Lights up another

Newport, gets on

the 405, blasts the 'Top

100' station, flips off

the speed-limit driver,

rejects the call

from her mother, gets off

the 405, parks the car

rear-in, lights another

Newport, watches the stray

tabby cat

risk its life

for food. At home,

she washes her
hands. Takes off
her bra, turns on
Netflix, throws out
the trash, warms up
her leftover falafels, listens
to her sister's voicemail, binges
on 'Scandal,' puts her phone
on Silent, sends her sister's
call to voicemail. In bed,

she prays
to herself, opens her night
stand drawer, stares
at the picture of herself at 7,
her father's hand
on her neck. She grips
her shoulder, squeezes

tight, her nostrils
flare, the bile resurfaces
to the back of her
throat, her nails

dig into her hand, callouses

don't let her bleed

anymore, just leaves

crescent-shaped imprints

in her palms. At night,

she doesn't cry. She washes

her hands.

Fog of Discontent

Felicia Taylor E.

Looking beyond her tiny kitchen door, she peered beyond the
white lace curtains

1960's butterfly brooch pinned upon the laced trim

Her aim was to fly beyond the stairway outside and to the pink
house chiseled into the Mountain View

But her fear was of those outside

Desiring the touch of something from them

Yet ushering them away with her prickly words and arthritic-ness
of her long finger curls

Once in the hospital, her neighbor came to visit "why are you here?"
She coyly demanded

The neighbor was taken by surprise, as her Good Samaritan duty
and efforts were being questioned

"You've never come to visit me at my home, yet you're here now.
Staring at me in my sickbed"

They never saw one another again

Not officially

But, in her home

peering through her covered windows,

being cloaked by her walls

And fog of discontent,

her fingers pined to touch someone

And arms ached to hold somehow

But the laciness of her soul only allowed fire to burn within her

Inside the decaying building she had created

Within a crippling space that she called Home

Little Bird

Ani Minasian

Remember the early days, little bird,

when you danced on the wind and

warbled under the late-night moon?

You didn't even know what you were

or what you were called

You had no name

but you were free

and natural

unrefined in your movements

but blissfully true

before you were trained

taught to respond to applause

before you had to earn your keep

and sleep in a cage

before they gave you a name:

Creativity

What are you now?

Paralyzed by restraints and judgment

You no longer fly

You've forgotten how to sing

Little old bird, is it Time

or the lack of

nature that's stolen your spirit?

If I release you back into the wild

will you thrive and sail again

on buoyant winds?

Will you fill the night

with your own brand of music

or have you fallen silent forever

unable to pluck yourself from the ground?

Tranquila y libre como el Buda
hay hacía desnuda
como recién nacida
toda desprendida - toda libertad
tierna doncella de Avándaro
pero ser libre así - sale caro
le secuestraron,
le torturaron,
le mataron a su maestro
Víctor Jara
la libertad sale cara

aqueya doncella se volvió ruda
se envolvía en lugares peores
que bares de mala muerte
con tal de no ser muda
la gente le llamaba indecente
los que la amaban no dudaban
en llamarla la más conciente
ya no más faldas y vestidos libres
ahora ropa negra apretada
mal portada con chalecos de cuero
con un acento un poco ñero

poco dormía y cuando lo hacía

era en jefaturas de policía

su vida pura anarquía

la libertad sale cara

ahora es tan popular y aceptada

como la Soda

ella se ve tan buena

ahora en video

como se escucha en Stereo

la doncella de Avándaro

a cambiado

un poco reggae y tropical

a si a regresado de aquella

Selva Negra

cambiada, pero toda integra

así es ella

libre y cambiante

y que Viva ,,,,, la doncella de Avándaro.

Titulo: La Doncella De Avándaro

Escrito Por: Abraham Jaramillo

The Turtle

Lois Jackson King

Go ahead and watch me, if that is what you must do

Just remember, I can see you too

Yes I do move a little slow, but I do make it to where I must go

Why should I be in a hurry

It will all be there whether it's today or tomorrow

Have you ever heard that haste makes waste?

I truly enjoy my slow and steady pace

As you watch me, you will surely see as I move forward

I do take the time to stop and look around

You might say I am taking a glance of this town

Not that there is anything unknown but seeing things from
    different angles

Will give me a broader picture of what has already been seen

I go from one place to another, viewing and reviewing

Seeing and re-seeing, evaluating and re-evaluating

Isn't that what life is all about?

The only thing that makes us want anything different

Is when we dare to compete within our own environment or
    society of

Them that want more stuff with less time to enjoy it

But let them have fun if they can, I'll just be me, the turtle slow
    and steady

Gray Area Longetivity

Michelle Smith

Mapamundi

Nery Martinez

7 continentes,

se devoran mis retinas,

7 años, la tarea me aburría,

Capitales,

cautivan mis pupilas,

Ciudades,

Calles rectas, calles curvas,

mi imaginación alucina

Imagina

Cambiar de norte a sur

de una a doble vía

Donde veo asfalto en desperdicio,

Una nueva ciudad, mi cabeza maquina,

27 años, mapas con crayón, con marcador, con tinta,

Cada noche, acumulo

Desde ese día.

leather-bound treasure map

Mauricio "Soul on Fire" Moreno

i find echoes in faded

ink, smell diffused sweat

clinging to brown napkins,

chicken scratch numbers written

with haste, long lost urgency:

lists of tasks, notes encroached,

jamming in between freeform writings,

slighting my pure

thoughts with blots

of sticky guilt.my journal holds

pieces of the puzzle

my shattered mind

cannot put together, so i jot

down my own morse

code, black skeleton keys

in the shape of cursive

letters. inside these paper

fibers, bindings of letters

strung together, i flip

each page back and forth,

an obsessed detective,

digging through mounds

of questions for answers.

why is mind so fucked

up, why can't i

complete a thought without mourning

for 100 others that never made

it onto the page?

why does every "7" have to have

a dash through it? because my grandfather

beat me when i didn't, because without it, it is naked,

vulnerable, something

i learned never to be.

why does my handwriting mix

between cursive and manuscript? because i

rebel against my mom's scolding, but not

all the way for fear of chaos,

structure-less, root-less,

truculent impulses.

why is my "M" in my last name

smaller than my first? because i

crave my own legacy

more than my fathers', though

i still honor his sacrifice,

but still besmirch it by

not claiming it for my own

why do i start every new sentence 1/2 an inch

further away? because i push

myself just a little more

away from middle ground, a half inch

closer to insanity, a half inch

closer to truth, a half inch

closer to my own sanity.

La Vida

Sanjui Martinez

Mexico,

My house, a one room building

With a kitchen attached

Where no hunger was felt

Not even the lack of love.

We were closer

Physically,

Spiritually,

Literally!

Sharing was a given:

Beds, clothes, toys.

You name it.

Amongst the ten of us.

One big meal

Prepared with love

Beans and tortillas

And chicken sometimes.

Because there was plenty.

Dad working forty hours

At 4.50 an hour

In the United States

Because he was a citizen,

Not the family.

Us, waiting for Fridays

To get our cheetos,

ice cream cups,

Or dark chocolate chips

by the bulk.

All from "el otro lado"

Oh what a joy!

Years past,

En los Estados Unidos

More rooms,

Isolation,

Sharing stopped

Because walls

Didn't allow it.

No more warm meals!

Mom went to work.

It is the U.S.

What do you expect?

Women have to work!

What a life!

Spring   little thing I let run beside me
the restless, unattainable,   fast me,
yet clumsy fuzzy ball couldn't keep the pace
not a race
I learned,   I learned a pack
doesn't arrive at different times

Summer   began to move like thunder
fast unpredictable youth
now   I   the one behind, harsh truth,
but much to learn the young Wolf needed
I the teacher, I the student, we the wanderer

Autumn   look at that Wolf
behaving amongst the sheep   must be a calm soul
behind every compliment there is a dog chasing a skunk
lessons stink,   yet
without them we are but a pup

Winter   slowly and steadily comes
back to the slower pace
          not a race
long walks into forests covered with snow
wise and tempered wolf, we blend into fog.

Title: Tala
By: Abraham Jaramillo

A Clean Pet

Lois Jackson King

I am thinking how nice and warm the water is, it feels so good

I want to splash around in the water and she wants me to keep still

"Stop now; you're getting water all over me"

Splashing here and splashing there,

Splashing water everywhere I did, I am sorry

Come on now don't be mad at me please just having fun

And soon we both will be out the door

How sweet I smell and how pretty I look

I am pretty enough to be in a picture book

Now she's the one that is a mess and has to take a bath.

My Cat Named Larry

Lois Jackson King

Hi diddle, diddle, the cat and the fiddle

Yea right, I don't want any other cat near my pillow

Once there was a living friend who I cherished til the end

He was a warm and gentle cat, but didn't put up with any mess

I learned this after having him a long time; being put to the test

One day, unexpectedly, I was outside, not far from where he was

A dog came to confront Larry, a dog more than twice his size

But it only made Larry's temperous character rise

What a fool thing to do, I thought to myself

The dog just stood there as to intimidate, so left them along to
do his thing

Facing the dog, he did not run, he was in the ring

There was no bell to ring, so to myself I sang

Get him Larry get him; just then Larry stood up on his back legs

He took a hold of a lower branch of a bush with one paw

With the nails from the other paw became longer

He struck out with a blow to that dog's face

Larry screamed out, with a loud cat (MEOW) growl

As if he was saying, take that; he gave that dog a couple of
good licks

That dog turned and went off running

Never to be seen again

Three shadows in the sky gradually descended into an alley. At first, a big and scruffy-shaped one made a harsh and heavy landing, followed by a tall and slender-shaped arriving a bit more gently a few hops back, and at last, a darker and smaller-shaped which stood on the edge of a trash can further from the body.

"Mike..!" the big crow screamed while flapping his wings in anger.

"Easy Fred," said the slender crow.

"Who could have done this to Mike?" the darker crow asked out loud from the rim of the trash-can where he was still perched.

"Who cares Ali. Whoever it is,,, is going to pay! You hear me, Eddy and Ali!" Fred yelled at his friends with anger and pain while circling and flapping his wings around the body of his friend Mike.

Eddy unfolded one of his wings and placed it on top of Fred. "Calm down, he was a great guy. We will find the punk who did this to him."

Just when Fred was calming down, the sound of a rolling food can, immediately followed by the sound of someone hiding between some rubble in the corner of the alley, rekindled Fred's fury. He started flapping and cursing towards that same direction.

Ali shrieked "Who is there!" He then began to fly up high to see who was hiding.

Meanwhile, Eddy was fallowing Fred while saying. "I got your back,,, I got your back Fred."

As they were getting closer to where the sound was coming from Fred shouted to the suspect of the murder of his friend Mike, "You will pay,,, you piece of..."

At the same time Ali, who was flying above and could now see everything, screamed. "NOOOOOO...!" as a big ginger cat was launching towards his friends.

Title: Murder No More
By: Abraham Jaramillo

Snowy Dragon

Nery Martinez

Sleepless night,

Tormenting roars and snores,

I couldn't cry alone in hell,

My own hell,

because of unwanted crowds,

Broke and hungry,

Took a bike,

in the freezing dark,

Could feel my fingers blue,

and my tears dry,

At City of Industry, I saw the waving flag

America, Land of dreams,

gave me a reason to keep the chain warm,

Leaving puffs of air, across warehouse land,

where drowned ducks lay, where no soul remains, but railway tracks

La Puente and Avocado Heights,

Desolate and far from home,

Alone but not for long,

As the wheels spun, the Snowy Dragon took off,

The San Gabriel Mountains covered up the sky,

I stopped and smiled. Encouraged to move on,

I stopped at a bridge overpass,

My eyes took a deep dive down, where one could hear the icy
water roaring into a rocky death trap,

There was a narrow sidewalk and a tiny metal fence at the edge.

There was wind whistling against the bridge.

There was me, facing an empty, unpredictable contraflow traffic
lane, but no one to run for help.

What I have done?

What I have done?

What I've always asked my whole life.

I didn't come here to die,

But my stomach growled, revindication stroke,

I turned to Snowy Dragon, so beautiful at last breath of dark.

Turned to it for love and protection, for understanding, and validation.

There it was.

Snowy Dragon melting at early dawn, mom's tears made me cry,

Dad's sharp thick eyebrows topped off the ice,

Look how they stare their only boy child,

I stared back at them,

If I died here, they would never forgive themselves,

but if I didn't try this far, I would never forgive myself,

I swallowed my balls, hit the pedal, biked over the narrow sidewalk,
pushed against the wind, shook at the edge of dawn,
from dark to bright. Crossed to the other side as the sun
warmed my way to El Monte.

To finish business in LA,

To come back home with a promise,

To come back and forever write.

Thanks Snowy Dragon, I still dream of you.

Coup

Nikolai Garcia

Jorge Martinez drank black coffee, and black coffee only. He never added sugar or creamer. He loved its bitter taste and hated the idea of flavored coffee. Whenever I saw him, he had a dark cup of coffee in one hand and a cigarette hanging on the edge of his mouth. I liked to read a lot, and we talked often at a bookstore where he worked, mostly about leftist politics. He considered himself a revolutionary and was staunchly against "electoral politics" (i.e. voting).

Jorge came from a country that experienced a different September 11; where the people elected a socialist as President—the first democracy in Latin America to do so. But it would not last, because Jorge also came from a country where the military staged a coup, dissolved the constitution, and disappeared (i.e. tortured and killed) over 3,000 of its citizens. For this reason, and for reasons that could only be understood by persons living in exile, Jorge had little faith in electoral politics.

Even so, it was hard for me to fully agree with Jorge's position. Although I loved the idea of revolution, I just could not see the masses of American people raising up in arms. "I just can't see it happening," was a common refrain on my part. It was at moments like this when butterflies came into the conversation. Jorge loved to bring up butterflies and their short life spans.

"Somewhere at this very moment," he would start, "there's a bright colored butterfly flying through a forest. It will suck the nectar from some flowers and then fly up and land on a branch. It will look around and say to itself, 'this is how it has always been, and this is how it will always be.'"

***

I lost track of Jorge after the bookstore closed its doors. I still read a lot, but I buy most of my books online now. I never really thought about him at all until this last election.

Two whole days had passed since election day, but there was still so much uncertainty. Key states that both nominees needed to win the presidency were still counting votes, so no one could officially call the election. And, although the Democratic nominee looked like he had the only clear chance of earning enough electoral votes to win the election, his Republican opponent would not concede the election. Not only would he not admit defeat, but he claimed the election results were a farce, that much voter fraud had been carried out by the opposing party.

Weeks later, after many recounts, after states certified their results, and the Democratic nominee was the clear winner, the sitting President would still not concede the election. He doubled down on the rhetoric and launched an army of lawyers to contest election results in any state where he could. But what was more alarming, was how he let loose his supporters to intimidate election officials. They protested outside their homes, most of them with guns, just because these officials had done their jobs.

It was then that my anxiety began to get the better of me. I was worried that something bad would happen. The word, "coup," began to pop into my mind continuously throughout the day. I made up scenarios of how this could happen, and I shared them with family, friends, and coworkers. But anyone who would hear my concerns would only laugh and say, "I can't see anything like that happening in this country." Despite what everyone told me, all I could think about was how the President could take control of the military and round up his supporters to defend his actions. (After all, 74 million people did vote for the guy)!

It's times like these that I wish I wasn't such a big reader, that I only cared about what next gadget to buy, or what I would watch next on TV. But, I find myself awake all night, with a cup of black coffee by my side, scanning article after article on the internet, checking to see if the word "coup" is mentioned anywhere.

Fists in the Air

Felicia Taylor E.

Thoughts turn to days

And days to months

I'm lost

Embedded within the expectations of an era of a People's fight,
a journey

For righteousness

I drove across town to stand up

speak up

Exist in a realm of shining a light within a bleak world

With a mask on, I parked and walked to a downtown gathering
of different minds that were alike

Fists in the air

Cries for justice

Against legalized murders

and suffering

Blue coats stood around, trapping us inside a barricade

Protection against us, pistols on their hip

As we stood with the weapon of our voice, strengthened by the
murdered souls that won't be silenced any longer

Black

      Lives

Brown

      Lives

Mattered

      matter

          forever

               will

Even when the civil war antiquities feel it's not truth

As we bowed our knees to the graveled ground in front of City
Hall, we prayed

Sang songs of reverence and hope

Moans overflowed with painful tears

as spy drones flew above us

Identifying, while picture snapping for the falsity to protect

I am of a people that fights

Strong stock's been brewed

Spirituals battling in this warfare

Minding and watching as those who have wronged, are in fear
of the prophecy

Watching,

as the tail becomes the Head

"Heads of State"

Struggles Are Real

Lois Jackson King

Uncertainties for all has become the norm

Unable to know will I be in position to tell tomorrow of today

Oh, do tell what power can reduce such strong, intense change

Will I receive a pink slip on life from another's hand

Inner-me, oh inner-me, give me hope on what I am to be

What influence can I truly voice which really sets souls free

Should I continue to muzzle the utterance of sound

Residency in spirit of love, compassion, knowledge of righteousness

Truths is yet to be seen of me; in the physical there is nervousness

Peace and justice can exist together; why can't mankind

Emotions of fear have moved in, and it's consuming

Many midnight hours of tears and heartfelt pain

Blocking from this stressful mess seems to remain

Oh inner-one, fight the force; will you stay facing the ground

Address the issue and turn your inner man completely around

There is no shame for you to be claimed, compassion is at hand

The shadow of fear, in spirit, has come, staring face-to-face

Enough frustration, bigotry, hate, injustice and crime

In leading, the outer man is from the strength of the inner man

Putting to death the intimidation of fear; a new confident
must appear

Not just for one, but for all mankind. Stand up and stand up straight

Fruitful in spirit and all that you say and do

A Vaporous Existence

Lois Jackson King

What is it that you have against me, where have I wronged you

What makes you torture me and nag me so

I don't come to you with my concerns that I can recall

So why do you approach me in this way

No matter where I go, you just have to show up

Wouldn't you like to be somewhere else

I can do without you being all up in my space

At any time, feel free to take a very long break

You are truly no use to me, as to where about I can see

You do have your strong points, but I don't know your purpose

You don't fit in. You can't be heard or seen, no shadow do you cast

What is your worth and are you truly welcomed

I am not a train, so get off and take all baggage

To you, I bid farewell, and goodbye; you are only a figment

I Bid Goodbye

Gustavo R. Ramirez

You are the clouds turned into gold.

I am courage. We are the bold.

I am the healing of my wounds.

We are the flowers about to bloom.

I am this moment in time.

Who am I?

I am the fury and the rage.

The wisdom of the sage.

I am loneliness and despair.

I am the people as they care.

You are the antidote to pain.

As I'm restored, I become sane.

You may believe that I'm in you.

I am the smoggy skies turned blue.

We say, "Farewell. Hello to plenty."

I bid goodbye.

I'm 2020.

toilet paper

Karyn Grasse

toilet paper

toothbrush

dental floss

hairbrush

sunscreen

eyeliner

house slippers

coffee mug

cereal bowl

running shoes

air pods

iPhone

eyeglasses

newspaper

clipboard

ink pen

iPad

refrigerator

microwave

paper towels

kitchen sink

laptop

cookie jar

notebook

tylenol

freezer

toaster oven

frying pan

wine glass

dish soap

vacuum cleaner

showerhead

warm towel

hair brush

dental floss

toothbrush

toilet paper

El Tiempo Cura?

Sanjui Martinez

Era el 2002.

Lucia bien a pesar del tiempo.

Pero qué falta de los dos!

Imaginar que la vida

era mejor alejados!!

Las quejas jamás cesaron.

La falta de edad, experiencia,

Un no sé qué apuntó

A lugares opuestos.

Y así empezó

O termino el comienzo.

Era el 2004.

Todo se pintó gris.

Una condena para todos.

Alambre de púas.

Dividiéndonos,

alejándonos

Por una decada.

Palabras medidas;

tres minutos X 5,

Con ansias esperadas.

Muchos holas y adios

Se sumaban.

Se pasaban el teléfono

Para ponerle más segundos

Al minuto.

Viajes de verano

A un lugar recluido

Nada parecido a la playa

O a la montaña.

Entrar era todo un lío.

Aun así,

Los corazones latían

Ansiosos por otro encuentro,

Miradas, abrazos

Muchos, muchos.

Mientras yo esperaba

El turno por si algo me tocaba.

Dos días, sábado y domingo

Visita especial

Donde con ingenuidad

Se entretenían

Con Juegos inventados

De fichas de botellas

De jugos, sodas,

En ausencia de juguetes.

El final del día

Se aproximaba

Y vendrían

Despedidas forzadas

Que destrozaban corazones,

Que rompían el alma,

Dolían mucho.

Sí. Dolían. Mucho.

Éramos los últimos en salir

Como queriendo alargar el tiempo.

Mientras las caritas

Lo seguían al alejarse

Y aún por el campo lo buscaban

Hasta desaparecer

Como quien espera ese avión

perderse entre las nubes.

Experiencias vividas

No se comparan

Pues después de eso

Hay que seguir otra vez

Con los brazos vacíos

En soledad

Un camino largo

Con ellos al lado.

Es 2020.

El tiempo cura, dicen.

Segun.

every self-help article i read on anxiety says—i need to break up with you.

Karo Ska

but i'm trapped

in our memories, how

we held clammy hands, how

my heart raced, how creamy & bitter

you tasted when i leaned my lips

in for a kiss. my body

vibrated whenever i consumed

you. oh, you made me feel

so good, my plumage bristling

with your energy. i miss

your smell—chocolate & forest, you

filled my house

with your presence. it's been

three months now,

& every time i pass

a cafe, i crave

the silk of your mouth

on my tongue. yesterday,

i opened my kitchen

cupboard & you

flirted with me, your smile

had me pulling you

out for a quick peck. you set

my mind ablaze & my toes

atingle. oh,

i missed you. aren't we

attracted to what makes us

feel good? each day

is hard without you. i'm addicted

to your warm

embrace in the mornings, but

i don't like how you make me

twitch & itch, how

you curl your claws

into my muscles, how you

make me forget to breathe, how

my thoughts are a broken

carousel whenever you're around. i'm tired

of the anxiety you provoke,

how i'm a mess

of bloody feathers after we make

love. i'm tired of your afternoon

crash, where i feel

sluggish & blurry. i know

it's best if we part ways, still

each day i think

about you, as i sip

my herbal tea, wondering what

you're doing & who

you're seeing. we're attracted

to what makes us

feel good, but that doesn't

mean it's good

for us. so i'm saying

farewell to you

for now.

One could clearly see the nature of his status in life
from the official and impeccable clothes he wore
to the four samurais who
fallowed him around - at all times
any peasant would have mind having such little
privacy,
but sadly his head needed no crown
to have a price on it,
his father made too many enemies,
which he paid by the blade of a woman
with revenge instead of pleasure on her head,
then, his older brother smother by
an assassin of the night,
yet this young Daimyo was of a different kind
physically of a slender complexion and defined
by his intellect and meticulousness,
he would not enter a room before it was checked,
he would not eat before the food was tasted,
he would not go a day without his routine,
wake up early to a warm tea,
then a walk to the garden
scare away any bee in the way of a flower he wanted
to smell,
then meet with people he had business with,
after all the formalities of the day
a well-deserved dinner while a musician played
was how he spend most of his days,

and so another day came,
and all of the sudden our young Daimyo
fell to the ground to the surprise of all around
the young Daimyo was purple dead, but how?
he would not enter a room before it was checked,
he would not eat before the food was tasted,
he would not go a day without these rules or
routines checked,
who could have guessed, the manner of his death,
who could have guessed, his everyday ways would
facilitate his untimely death,
for his closest people found   Poison
Poison on the beautiful flowers ,
the beautiful flowers he smelled every day.

Title: Daimyo's Way
By: Abraham Jaramillo

Cry Me a River

Felicia Taylor E.

Tired of You playin' with my heart

Throwing darts at my spirit as you

speak,

lie,

talk

Coming back with endless love and possibilities

That never yield me any closer to respectability

Defined my feelings, "like the silliness of a child"

But you don't treat me that way when the lights are out

I'm done with the wine me, dine me and toss

me to and fro'

You'd best get movin' fore' this smoke stack burns you up

I'll prove to you, how strong I am

Come back and speak to me again?

You'll cry me a River and really be alone

I'll watch those flames,

the whole night long

Imagination Running Amok

Lois Jackson King

Be smart you careless fool and be wise

I surely shouldn't have to be told twice

My life can be surprisingly cut too short for me to be "a fiend"

Can my life not be hidden; everything I do can it be seen

Why can't it be said, he throws the ball and hid his hand

Why must assumptions be; all my deeds known to man

Come you, and walk with me, we will sit right here

Let no one see us; have a drink or two without fear

We must be still as those stones around us, they just might hear

Enjoying it all I say, like, loud music which makes life real

They meant no harm; where did the blood come from

Torment, it seems so true, oh, what will to do

You might just get by, cut me some slack; get away

Don't be foolish, running and letting the flesh lead you astray

Truth, reality comes and goes; smoke stream of it all

Nightmares during the day; sweet inner spirit on you do I call

For if not now, surely you'll come at the end

Emotion, emotions, oh so real, but victory is to win

I.See.You.

Luz Donis

Why do you have to be so

intense? You never used to be

this way. Before

you used to know

when it was time

to let go.

You used to be

so caring.

I.See.You.

It all changed when you went high

tech. I met you

in the 90's. Remember

how freaked out we were

when El Sida hit us

hard. We lost too many...

All you ever think about

is quantity

not quality.

When will you ever learn?

I.See.You.

Don't you dare forget,

when you're done with them,

they come down

to me. Some

like Humpty Dumpty.

Ok, so what! I wipe away

the tears, the snot

and hold a hand.

The likes of a Nightingale

walk my shiny scrubbed

floors day and night.

I.See.You.

So where does that leave you

and your heroic measures?

You're up to your ears fighting

that bitch 'Rona with La Catrina

riding you and rattling

her bones. Why do you have to be

so fucking intense.

Defeated

Karyn Grasse

Your elbow, a 7th grade acute

angle, digs into my side

and doesn't let

up, I can smell your hot

breath, feel it on the fringe

of hair at the nape

of my too pale neck, as you twist

my hands into snarled

shapes into my back

flesh. Your hands—your

hands black and cold—move

too fast, solid lines that I

cannot bend to my will. You

laugh at me with those

hands as you throw your full

weight triumphantly onto

my torso, pinning me into

the mat sweat, sealing my

defeat. you bend

your round face close, so

close, to my red

and burning ear, so

close the canal tingles

with your vibrations as

you

whisper

"tick-tock"

Battle of Power

Lois Jackson King

What number can we put the phrase, early childhood; how can the inner be separated from the outer, is that an answer, where can they run for help, and who can they tell when there is fear in their heart

Run, run, and more running; but is there a hiding place? Please don't hit me, no more, "ouch" is a mild word for all the many moments of physical pain that can't be expressed in words alone

Not even the inner man can change the reality which the eyes see and the evil word to be heard. It's too… … … much for one to take, just too… … … much

Mistakes after mistakes, over and over again and then some; give it up, please. I am on my begging knees; turn away, turn away. Now it's so… … … bad with this driven force of action

What is in the bottle anyway? Can I wish on a star and make it go away. Now here come "The Man" dressed in their fine blue, driving their two-tone mobile, giving out the warning, "This… … … has got to stop"

"Get it together or you will have a new resident with only a P.O. Box number." Compiled by drinking and a mind fogged up; activate unbalance in thinking straight

Put down the glass and the bottle, you must throw away fleshly desire out the window now. Breaking from which has wrongly directed your to do, now I can see a brand new you. Oh, how I thank God for you making loving life new

No more object control over you; no more running trying to hide myself from all the physical pain; now you are the one who is in control. I am able to be embraced by love and compassion, a new norm, a new mom, and a new life ever so sublime

Conformed

Lois Jackson King

Mess after mess, what are we doing to each other; where is the family love. I don't see, nor do I feel, what should be in place. Keeping calm, I do pray a lot for their peace. We have the same relatives, same household and mom.

Am I the strange one, a long way from a normal life, why do they dis me until they are in need; fussing, fussing, that's all they do. Ring, ring sounds from the phone, "Come quick, they at it again. Put it down, no, no, stop, stop." is what I hear.

Love of family, can make you do some crazy things. Should I go because the call came in? What could the matter be, anxiety is setting in me. Traffic is too slow; I hope they have stopped before I get there. Heart racing fast, but I must be calm.

Police out front, front door open, "I didn't mean to do it; I didn't." Blood rush to my head; in an outrage, acting like a mysterious monster from the Black Lagoon. The qualities of an untamed beast have appeared, abnormal behavior in every way.

Anger and displaced frustration has overshadowed. Long trails of tight chains has now been broken; the... ... has hit the fan. A fire ablaze, please, please, please bring me some water, I prefer the historical.

East is East and West is West, and the two will never, ever meet. "So shall I say parting is a wonderful thing to behold?" No more range over me; we can't choose relatives, but we can choose family; I have learned the difference; and with sanity in its rightful place.

MD

Mauricio "Soul on Fire" Moreno

She knows how to manipulate

her words to achieve

what she wants. Behind her

sincere smile and curly

locks is a wizard, master in the arcane

arts of gab. Her words

are never straight, they curve in another

direction, always leaning

towards suspicion, a subliminal

incline into smugness. Her words

are never black

or white. They have a shade

of gray mixed within

their meanings, a sliver of silver

guilt adorning every syllable,

a tingle of pain

in every tilde, a puff

of venom in every shallow

breath. The strength robbed

from her aging body
replaced by a keen
awareness, a wit sharp
as blades as she cuts

through my pride
with precise palabras. A subtle
change in her timbre to demand

submission, an octave
higher to feign weakness, a lithe
pinch of guilt to conquer
my logic. She knows
what to say to make me

believe it was my idea, her own
words embedded in my
vernacular, etched
in every sound. But she doesn't

know that I have
resented her
in secret. Behind my persona

of good son, I've held a fire

inside to define

my life, not by her

standards but my own. So much so

that I have crafted

every layer of defense

with reasoning

and patience, logic

with a smile, to make her

believe I am still

under her spell. But she doesn't

know that I have

spotted every sleight

of tongue in her daily

calls. Every time

I nod my head, I hide my doubt.

And every time she thinks

she wins, I continue

with my own plan. Today,

she wished me well

in class, her wish

sprinkled with dust

of enchantaje for not

speaking to her longer. I thank her,

hang up the phone, and continue

with my online class.

Ouch Grandma, That Hurt!

Lois Jackson King

When it came to spanking, grandma pulled down those pants

She didn't mind the dirt, works for the ants

Three peach tree limbs, which she made into a braid

Crazy mixed words she would say, "It hurts me more than it hurts you"

Those spankings helped me to do what I needed to do

"I am doing this to give you character; because I love you"

Oh so true; building character for the outside with her hands of love

Giving strength to my spirit; but did she have to love so hard

Experiencing work with grandma: day's work, it was called

There was no shame; she held her head up nice and tall

Cleaning many things; making beds and cleaning floors

"Get an education and I want you to please stay in school

So you'll be able to accomplish greatness and not be fooled"

Grandma taught me how to cook

Her cooking skill was not from a book

Many years for the railroad, she had cooked

I learned as I watched, it's easy as I took a look

I will always remember my grandma who was ever so grand

Her guiding hands developed character and degrees in my plan

Matriarch

Sanjui Martinez

She did things differently.

Fifty five years lived by his side.

He did everything for her.

Worked hard all his life,

Like men in his time would do.

"Women are to stay home," he would say.

And she would peacefully accept.

"Not for me!"

I would quietly say.

Guela never disagreed.

She spent all her life

Serving, loving, following

This man, mi Guelo Pancho,

To the end of the world.

She was not the one who made decisions.

She simply followed.

She cooked his meals, washed his clothes

Never complaining about life.

Then her world collapsed.

Guelo Pancho fell ill.

In eight months,

lost all she had worked hard for:

Keep this man happy and well fed.

In just eight months, he succumbed.

Gone.

What was she to do now?

Stop living?

No, my grandma kept on.

Not the same, of course.

But she didn't give up.

Eight children,

With three boys at home, she changed her skirts

To pants and carried on.

With an iron fist, that is,

She decided to live.

She raised them to be men of character,

just like Guelo would.

And in her was an inner strength that her daughters inherited.

She ruled her home, kept the family glued

By cooking her soul food: arroz con pollo.

This is how she made her house

the setting of my childhood memories.

She lived.

Yes, she lived a fulfilling life

And passed it on to us.

And now, thanks to her, I live to tell.

For Even to the end of her days,

She remained faithful to us, to him.

Even on her deathbed, she called for him

To come take her with him for her life on earth was done.

Ay Guela, la matriarca, Gracias!

Being Truthful

Lois Jackson King

The great composer and singer, James Cleveland, sung the song "I Don't Feel No Ways Tired" inspired by an enderly woman who walked down a rough and dusty road for many years.

Her only way to get from one place to another. And when she was asked what was it which gave her endurance and motivation to walk miles, year after year, her reply was, "not getting tired of doing what is needed to be done, but what you alone must do." Even though I haven't had to travel in her footsteps down the same old dusty road.

The passion I have, and strong determination, to keep going forward and the will to reach beyond all of the challenges. I too don't feel no ways tired, "Cancer of 1983, you tried your touching way, did it get you what you want? Hey you, no buddy of anybody, and still up to your touches. Yes, you returned in 1986, defeated once more and again."

Can it be that I am a vessel which is fed up with you; a representation of a foot out the door of health and the strength of life. Facing uncertainties of life, I lose not, for strength is gained through the power of victories claimed.

Victory is leading the way, I am not far behind, get out of the path. Continue to be beaten, as you were created to. You are history; no faking, you actually pushing up daisies. My, my, my.

Hello Victory, thank you for your perseverance into my affairs.

Can you feel me? I don't feel tired, I am determined to continue on. Who is at the door now? Don't ask if you can come in; you already have your feet in the way. Well, Victory, you allowed me to come through; and by the Grace of God I am able to keep my sight, even though it is impaired after four necessary operations, but we are best of buddies, and I have the victories of an abundant life.

World winds, world winds; it is summery time. Life is a journey; technology on our side. Not one, but two replaced hips, woo, woo, and a replaced knee. Yea, and I am doing what is best. And to God I leave the rest. Come in spirit of mind, if nothing else works, "He, He, He," and remember this, "I Don't Feel No Ways Tired."

Magnifico'

Felicia Taylor E.

My soul moans with each ounce I'm given for you

Rhythmic beats come to me as we prance

African calypso, Salsa style or Gospel cabaret

I become a fluffy bit of headedness in your midst

Intoxicated by your aromatic scents and enticement of spices

Your whip appeal as Babyface states is unnerving to say the least

Ha-ha!

In finality, we erupt as one

Sharing and showcasing our magnifico' status of yumminess!

He is Alpha and Omega

Lois Jackson King

Unique in every way; no one to compare

Nature of compassion never changed will be there

Stooping down to lift you up; the wisdom which is spoken will
brighten your way

Wisdom with hope and the courage to stand, and meet
challenges of life and not stray

Without fancy words and false dreams; just true revelation of all
the facts

Working with so many others is part of the reality; real in all things
and not a fake

Nature motivates and is of the strongest of love from the heart

Both transcendent and immanent; tower over all and is supreme

Love is eternal; no interest in material things or important names

Building without help of a fabricated blueprint is the ability

The distinctive qualities and attributes with faithfulness is every plan

Unchanging in His ways and continuing to work things right

With power of adequacy to meet the needs is a personal fight

Continuing involvement in the life of all mankind; never to
leave alone

From the above nature just described, many episodes in one's life

Our understanding of one thing is very different from that
of another

Who is it you wish you could be; will love spoken change you or me

You do you, and let me do me; my character reflects the
spiritual tree

Good bad or indifferent

You or I are not God; there is no perfectness in us

It is to be found; what you see is what you get

The Star

Michelle Smith

A New Me

Lois Jackson King

My outer appearance is deceiving; the face, is just like a clown

My inside emotions can't be seen when others are around

The me I present seems to be turned upside down

I have low self-esteem; yes my spiritual face has many frowns

Outer appearance, it's like a mask; like fake news, flowers or grass

And the way that I am, I can't blame anyone; I don't move fast

I want you to come and look a little closer, get to the know the
real me

My name is "Self." The "S" for shyness; the "E" for emotional
guilt and pain

The "L" for the physical limp I have; the "F" for faith which keep
me going forth

With character building classes, I have the assurance that everything
will be alright

The outside forces have lost their strength; the reality of life
motivates my spiritual fight

Even though, most of the time, I live my life with very little sound

Because emotionally, I rather be up, instead of being
spiritually down

As the uncertainty of life comes to face to face, I will push forward

I now speak with experience and authority; only the outer was
responded to

Many things may not change, but facing reality, I must to my
self be true

From this moment on, my inside is not the picture of the inside;
I will be brand new

Love Portion

Lois Jackson King

Love, for us, will be a wonderful and beautiful way

No matter the ups and downs or the many challenges, it won't lead us astray

Vision eternally, the fire of passion never to burn out; side by side to stay

Continuing to embrace, the presence of you, being in my space

Memories boxed; fragrance lingers; music summons you to me

So many have put claim on you; are you being really true

Games of lies and deceit must not exist; thought always on you

"In the Still of the Night" by the Five Satins, ponders my mind

Many words to express my thoughts, the nearness is sublime

A made up mind; not confused about the way that I feel

Says "Promise I'll never let you go" for me, love is real

Welcome to my receiving heart; for in love is where I am at

Atmosphere of love is beautiful, and that's a fact

Hell Love!

Nery Martinez

Hello...

Hell Love!

Missing what we were

Missing what we could've been

Hello...

Hell Love!

Not forever love,

but forever pain,

Deleting one pic at the time,

one message after I sigh,

Not yet ready,

But still trying,

Still whispering,

Hello...

Hell Love!

Nice kiss!

Nice to meet you, stranger...

Pizza

Mauricio "Soul on Fire" Moreno

You kneaded me,

tried to shape me

to your liking, extra-thin

crust, light sauce, easy

on the toppings, bland.

Your well-intentioned hands

smashed my skin, spread

emotions evenly on

a cold surface.

Like a child, you tossed me

in the air, filled my body

with hope, weightless,

dead space underneath

me, knowing you

would catch me.

You shut me in,

claimed you were helping

me grow, locked away

from others, because I was

not ready.

Not ready

to show the creation

your two hands

made from nothing.

Not ready

to claim me as your precious

gift to the world.

I listened to you,

gave your opinion

precedence over my desire

to grow. I cauterized

my ambitions,

let my insides

simmer and bubble.

I constructed my own oven,

shut the world out,

because you said I was

not ready.

I let your love

burn me, char

my insides. My flavors
trapped in my blackened
crust. My gifts melted,
my talents crumbled,
lost for anyone to
taste, except for you.
Because you said I was
not ready

But this fire was never yours.

My flavors were never
yours to claim, they were
gifts from my ancestors,
exotic flavors, fermented wisdom,
esoteric, complex.

You couldn't distill
my essence with your logic
and science. My recipe
came from hands that
worshipped soil, honored
the sun, bled rituals from
their veins.

You thought you were

the head chef,

and I your Michelin star.

But you were only

a taste-tester, barely

capturing the complexity

of my flavor.

Passion But No More Kisses

Nery Martinez

Passion at the first kiss

Love at the second kiss

But… Fear at the third kiss?

Why?

Who hurt you so bad?

Who else than me to clean up the beats

of what seemed to be a beating heart?

Why?

Why give me a chance?

A chance to give and receive love,

to be kicked out of a stranger's house?

Sorry to invade,

your little fortress of shame,

your fortress of loneliness,

your fortress of love denial,

your fortress of self-punishment.

Reflections of Hope

Lois Jackson King

The desire of more peace encamps the mind, and is filling the heart

Seeking a little breeze of compassion; meanwhile abuse is stuck
in park

Running away from strife; full bundles of hostility

Looking for a bit of comfort; reaching out in humanity

Showing by example, how to give and not eager to take

Helping to do that which is right; giving all mankind an even break

Moving, in love, a sense of justice; looking toward the higher mark

Operating as a light in the midst of all surrounding darkness

Trying hard to reflect His likeness and image in times of harshness

Cruelty and mistreatment is at large; with power trampling

Causing hurdles and droves of pain; creating a spiritual thinning

Over shadowing the reality of love, which was in the beginning

But with continued hope, hopefully will soften the hunk

Council of the heart; remembering His promise, I will not flunk

No shame in clinging to that which gives strength to reach…
… upward

Where the… … "Spirit" meets emotion and smooths a bumpy road

In all that I am and desire to be, it's the hope that makes me free

Nights of many tears and the days equal with pain

Through it all, yes, I have come; the mind of others can't
be explained

Continuing in "Hope" is my desire and will continue to be my aim

Esa Mentira

Gustavo R. Ramirez

Una mentira que destruye

        Es peor que matar.

Porque si te matan

Ya no sientes nada

        Y puedes descansar.

Pero esa mentira que destruye

Te mata el alma.

Te parte el corazón.

Te destroza

    Cada momento,

      Día tras día,

        Año tras año

          … una eternidad

That Lie

Gustavo R. Ramirez

A lie that destroys

                    Is worse than killing

For if they kill you

You don't feel anymore

                    And you can rest.

But that lie that destroys

Kills your soul.

It shatters your heart.

And tears you apart

    Each moment,

        Day after day,

            Year after year

                … an eternity

Return to Sender

Mauricio "Soul on Fire" Moreno

I find the courage to

write to you again.

My questions scatter on

composition paper like black

marbles, crashing into white

barriers.

I grip the pen with numb fingers,

ripping through the paper,

black crosses and slashes

adorning my Religion notebook.

The ticking bomb between

my ears threatens to explode

if I don't diffuse the words into

light blue wires on the page.

I ask for forgiveness,

for waking you up

when I called the nurse

a bitch.

for scaring you,

when I slammed the door

to your room.

for not being there, when

they took you off the respirator.

I ask if you're doing all right,

tell you about suicide, about

the flowers left for you.

I rant about our padres,

how it was unfair that

you didn't get a chance.

I ask if He ever cared

to answer my questions,

or if he just left them on 'Seen.'

I wasn't sure of your address

so I wrote down 'Heaven'

added three stamps, just in case,

dropped it off before school.

I get your letter back.

Return to Sender.

Insufficient Address.

Unable to Forward.

I wish the Post Office tried harder.

Bad Muse

Lois Jackson King

Continually being urged by you, all up in my space, here and there, even in my love affair. Do you mind if in my mind I turn aside from your meddling? What interest do I hold for you spending time with me, it is so overwhelming, don't you get it, I am tired of you?

I am fed up with your idealistic way of thinking and twisting things about. I look in the mirror, I also have knowledge of my qualities, and I don't need feedback from you. To be honest, it is I who can help you, and others like yourself, to become the best you can truly be.

And while I am on a roll, what credentials do you hold for your insight into… … … my self-exploration; are there secret documents that is held in favor of you; is it a fair assumption that you know me… … … as well as I know myself, and if so, what are your intentions?

Impulse seems to be your game, no pacific aim; a few other things I could name. But I am standing up to you… … face-to-face, no more shucking and jiving and unused mind controlling trash.

Pushing you way back so far in the rear, I'll be covering all of your tracks; most defiantly from now, there will be only one way of doing things.

It will be my "Mind," yes it will be mine as well. Only one set of footprints in my sand of life. I will be seen as a free, single "Spirit," a free, fresh spirit I shall truly be; oh so free for the world to see.

A Gift

Nery Martinez

Death is a gift

she mumbles

Fever spikes,

I sweat, hallucinate and hydrate

Sip a coffee

She joins, she sits

I crack my knuckles

You ready?

Maybe, more coffee?

She sees me with empty eyes,

I go and kiss her empty mouth,

Huh, you want the easy way out?

No rush! She pushes me out

I bounce against my pillows,

Air blows through my eardrums,

I'm alive,

First I cry,

but give thanks to see the sunshine

You see?

Life is a gift,

she mumbles.

Summoning Demons

Nikolai Garcia

The restroom was located adjacent to the football field. It was a semi-abandoned building that the school only opened during football games. The fact that there was no power inside the place made it the perfect location to use my newly acquired Ouija board. It was dark, but not spooky, as there were plenty of windows that brought in the bright Los Angeles sun.

Diana, a thin, curly-haired girl, who never hung out with us, kept looking out the windows. She was not the type to ditch class, and only agreed to join us after being peer-pressured by my girlfriend, Vero. When she saw school security approach the building where we were hiding, she immediately wished she had gone to algebra class.

Julio, who was a year older—and therefore wiser—than the rest of us, was quick to react. He knew how much trouble we would all get into if they had found any marijuana on us, so he flushed what little we had not smoked down the toilet. (We had smoked most of it already so it wasn't a huge loss).

Dopey, (who was given that nickname in middle school on account of his large ears), was quick to overreact. He did not want to get caught, so he ran around the bathroom desperately looking for another exit. Watching him was more annoying than it was amusing. We had escaped school security plenty of times before, but today would not be one of those days. Dopey was able to reach the small windows above the sinks, but they had metal bars on the outside, so no way to crawl out of them. This place was pretty much a death trap (and probably one of the reasons we weren't supposed to be in there).

To make matters worse, one of the security guards that was on his way to catch us was a guy named Derrick. We all hated him and called him, "Hootie," behind his back. (We gave him this nickname on account of his strong resemblance to Darius Rucker, the lead singer of the 90s one-hit wonder band, Hootie and the Blowfish). We had recently escaped his clutches by jumping over a fence, so he had been waiting to catch us fucking up.

I knew it would not go well for me once I got home, but I tried to keep my cool as much as I could. I wanted to comfort my girlfriend. She and Diana held hands together in a corner, tears forming in their eyes. She was terrified of what her mom would do to her. She was not a goody two-shoes, but she also had never been caught in a dark bathroom playing Ouija. We didn't even get to start the game, but as far as anyone was concerned, we were devil-worshipping youth, doing drugs and summoning demons.

Oscar sat on the floor, tracing the Nike swoosh on his black and white Cortez, waiting for the security guards to come through the door. He hadn't attended any of his classes in weeks and he knew he was facing serious discipline from the school dean. But, I once saw him have a fist fight with his own father, so I knew he wasn't worried about the consequences. When Derrick walked in and instructed us to get in a straight line and follow him to the dean's office, Oscar got up and said, "Lead the way, Hootie." We didn't contact any spirits or summon any demons that day—and we all got into trouble—but seeing Derrick's face flush with anger when Oscar spoke back to him almost made it all worth it.

Still Haunted

Tina Fallon

I'm still haunted, I'm still haunted by the treatment

When I see someone who has lost focus and then suddenly brought back to their senses by the abrupt voice of their manager/counterpart, I am there again.

The constant blame for anything that went wrong.

For the boasting of how much her partner makes and the shoes she buys with her own money. When stilettos were a thing and also when they were not.

I had to climb over boxes looking for some stupid thing that didn't matter.

While you attended the event dressed to the nines sucking up compliments. Parasite.

"I never eat dinner… ha ha ha, I used to be chubby," Anything to keep her 105lbs at a constant. Later to find out she was talking about a mere 15lbs. And family members called her gorda, even after the weight loss.

In dreams, I'm back in that building—1933 South Broadway.

Wandering the halls of almost every floor. Sometimes there's an event going on and every showroom is lit to their own unique theme. Christmas, Romantic, Elegance, Sophistication, and Whatever.

Sometimes the old showroom is filled with weird and odd merchandise: rugs, lamps, piles and piles of never before seen fabric while the song, "Here I Go Again" by Whitesnake is played. And I'm not a fan.

In real life, I felt abused and beaten. I felt like I let it happen. I blame myself. She always gave me things like food, clothing and money. Like I was her property. Then there was the time we were getting off the plane at LAX from a long flight. A work conference. Can't remember if it was early morning or late at night. Tired. Just tired. We were sitting together. I got up first because I was closest to the aisle. I made my way to the exit, yet I was moving slowly. Then, suddenly I felt a hand push me on my back! Unbelievable! How dare she… But nothing. Nothing to be done. I just teared up and let it pass.

Secreto Al Mar

Sanjui Martinez

Otra vez se le vio llegar

a la orilla del mar

aquel día de invierno

como cada año.

De su mochila

Sacaba una foto

que apretaba

contra su pecho

mientras cerraba los ojos.

Por las pocas prendas

que cubrían su piel,

titiritaba de frio.

Pero ni eso la alejó.

Veía hacia el horizonte,

suspiraba hondamente,

buscando no sé qué.

Esperando no sé qué.

Lucía en su rostro

con cierta elegancia

algunos 60 otoños

que delataban la belleza

que ya se le había ido.

Sus cabellos plateados

le adornaban la sonrisa

que una vez tuvo.

Sus ojos cafes claros,

focos apagados de su alma,

encerraban un secreto

difícil de decifrar.

Y solo se sabia

que era de un lugar lejano.

Que llegó con poco equipaje,

sin sonrisa alguna,

y una mirada perdida,

que hablaba con las aves

cada vez que podía.

Y así se fue…

oprimiendo el cuadro

hacia su pecho,

con la mirada ida.

Titiritando.

Suspirando.

Y así, como Alfonsina Storni,

caminó hacia el mar.

La diferencia—

Su secreto se lo llevó al mar.

About the Authors
Sobre los autores

Tina Fallon

Tina Fallon has a Bachelor of Arts for Drama from Cal Poly Pomona and a partial associates in Child Development from VVC. Her favorite authors are Stephen King, Edger Allan Poe, Zadie Smith, John Ajvide Lindqvist, Amy Sedaris, Amy Poehler, Amy Schumer, Tina Fey and David Fallon. She lives with her husband, David and son James in Victorville.

Karo Ska

Karo Ska uses poetry and art to flush out the contradictions of this Western-imperial society. She hopes to threaten the status quo and build towards an anti-authoritarian, autonomous world. She questions the legitimacy of the Amerikkkan empire and recognizes Los Angeles as Tongva Territory.

Nery Martínez, Jr.

Nery Martínez, Jr.; writer of stories, poetry, and more. His experiences flourish in his words and tales, presenting to us a world that is often troubled, but always full of hope.

Karyn Grasse

Karyn is a Monterey Park native and has been writing short stories and poems since she was 12. Sometimes, they get published. Sometimes, they sit in a box. Her most treasured creative endeavor, however, is the charming little person who has invaded her life for the past several years.

Lois Jackson King

Mother of 4 with 11 grandkids, 10 great grandkids. Her writings encourage and inspire, while some may have you laughing aloud.

Abraham Jaramillo

Abraham Jaramillo is a multimedia artist; illustrator, graphic designer, and photographer. His love for the arts began back when he created small sketch galleries for his grandmother when he was 8 years old. A longtime volunteer and teaching artist with DSTL Arts, Abraham enjoys and nurtures the pursuit of knowledge both in himself and others.

Mauricio Moreno (Soul on Fire)

Mauricio is an artist and writer, originally from the East Coast. He moved to California to fulfill his life mission of being a writer and sharing the stories of others to bring readers closer together and heal the world. He is currently working on a novel under the mentorship of Nicolás Obregón and is also in the process of publishing his first collection of poetry.

Felicia Taylor E.

Felicia Taylor E. joins the Conchas y Café family for the first time in this issue. Their contributions to this zine illustrate a love for life, justice, and the written word.

Luz Donis

Second generation Guatemalan, raised in Boyle Heights. Trained and worked as a nurse for L.A. County and L.A. Unified. Currently immersed in Vipassana meditation and Buddhist studies.

David Fallon

In the early 2000s, David Fallon published a handful of plays, poems, and stories. He took a 10 year sabbatical to build a career and raise a son. The recent death of his mother prompted him to return to writing– primarily short stories and an upcoming novel.

Jessica V. Gonzalez

Born and raised in Toledo, OH. Grew up in N.E.L.A. Grew out in South Central. Mother of two, and blessed to have found Conchas y Café to get me back into the one consistent thing with all the moves… writing.

Sanjuanita Martinez

Sanjuanita joins the Conchas y Café family from The Valley. A poet and educator, Sanjuanita writes from the heart, in the language that comes first, the language that best represents her voice.

Michelle Smith

Michelle Smith is a poet and artist working toward producing work that emits love and empathy for people of all kinds. She is a welcome addition to our Conchas y Café Zine family of artists.

Ani Gohar Minasian

Ani Gohar Minasian is a Los Angeles-based Armenian-American singer and writer of poetry, songs, plays, and prose. She earned a Bachelor of Theatre Arts from Cal Poly Pomona and has taught English and creative writing to middle and high school students. She is passionate about nurturing young talent, supporting other artists, and advocating for the fair representation of Armenian culture in mainstream media. animinasian.com

Nikolai Garcia

Nikolai Garcia was raised in South Central; lives in Compton; and works in East Hollywood. He is Associate Editor for Dryland. His first chapbook, "Nuclear Shadows of Palm Trees," published DSTL Arts, is out now.

Gustavo Reyes Ramirez

With an activist heart and yearn for building commnunity, Gustavo Reyes Ramirez writes, writes, and writes. His first self-published collection of poetry is available now.

About the Conchas y Café program

Conchas y Café is a 12-week workshop series for adults, focusing exclusively on creative writing, literacy, and illustration. Participants have the opportunity to work with volunteer writers and artists on developing artwork that will be published and presented in a triannual 'zine and public reading.

For more information, locations, and dates for upcoming Conchas y Café workshops, contact us by email at *info@DSTLArts.org*.

Acerca el programa Conchas y Café

Conchas y Café es un taller de 12 semanas para adultos, especializando en escritura, literatura, y dibujo. Participantes tienen la oportunidad de trabajar con escritores y artistas voluntarios en el desarrollo de obras de arte que serán publicados y presentados en publicaciones trimestrales y lecturas públicas.

Para más información, localidades, y fechas de próximos talleres de Conchas y Café, contáctenos por correo electronico al *info@DSTLArts.org*.

This program is supported in part by:

This publication was produced by DSTL Arts.

DSTL Arts is a nonprofit arts mentorship organization that inspires, teaches, and hires emerging artists from underserved communities.

To learn more about DSTL Arts, visit online at:

DSTLArts.org

 @DSTLArts

 /DSTLArts